FOSS Science Stories

Human Body

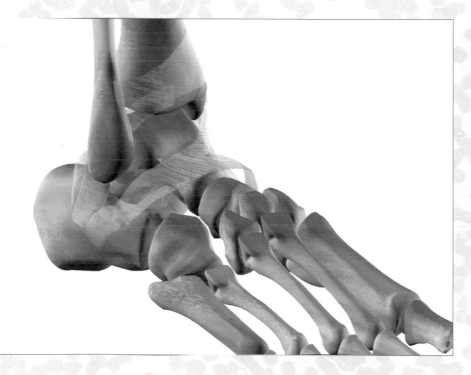

Developed at

Lawrence Hall of Science

University of California at Berkeley

Published and Distributed by **Delta Education**

ISBN 1-58356-841-7

542-2006

2 3 4 5 6 7 8 9 10 QUE 09 08 07 06 05 04

TABLE OF CONTENTS

Capillaries are thin, tiny blood vessels that carry blood through the tissues.

Veins carry blood back into the heart. Veins are thinner than arteries. Blood moving into the heart moves with less pressure than blood coming out of the heart.

BLOOD

Blood is a lot more complex than you might think. Your blood is made up of different types of cells.

Red blood cells carry oxygen through the body. Your body makes millions of red blood cells every day. There are about 6 million red blood cells in a small drop of blood.

White blood cells fight infection in the body. There are about 10,000 white blood cells in a small drop of blood.

Platelets are tiny cell pieces that cause blood to *clot*, or stick together. When you get a cut or scrape, the platelets clot. This prevents you from losing too much blood. There are about 400,000 platelets in a small drop of blood.

Plasma is a clear, yellow liquid. It carries nutrients and proteins throughout the body. Half of your blood is made up of plasma.

Heart

Lungs

Veins

Arteries

GLOSSARY

Ball-and-socket joint A place where the rounded end of one bone fits into the cup of another bone. Ball-and-socket joints allow movement in two directions, in addition to rotation.

Bones The individual parts of the skeleton.

Cartilage The smooth, flexible material that connects some bones and provides shape for some body parts.

Contract To become smaller or shorter in length.

Exoskeleton Any hard outer covering that protects or supports the body of an animal.

Fracture A break in something, especially a bone.

Gliding joint A place where two bones meet, allowing limited movement in two directions.

Hinge joint A place where two bones meet, allowing movement in one direction.

Joint A place where two bones come together.

Ligament Tissue that connects bone to bone. Ligaments often guide the direction of tendons, especially in the wrist and hand.

Muscle Tissue that can contract, producing movement.

Organ A structure of the body that performs a particular function.

Skeleton The hard inner framework of bones inside an animal that provides shape, support, and protection.

Skull The hollow case of the head made up of fused flat bones and moveable jaw bones. The skull surrounds and protects the brain, inner ears, and eyes.

Suture The joint or line formed by the closure of two skull bones.

Tendon Ropelike tissue that connects muscle to bone.

Tissue Any of a number of different kinds of materials that make up the body, such as muscle, tendon, ligament, and bone.

A MARVELOUS MACHINE

One of the most marvelous machines in the world is the human body. The many parts of your body work together, allowing you to walk, run, jump, and play. Even while you sleep, the body keeps working.

Your skeleton is an important part of you. It is the framework of the body and gives the body its shape. As you grow, your skeleton grows and changes with you. Your bones grow, and some even fuse together. By the time you are 1 year old, your skeleton has about 200 different bones.

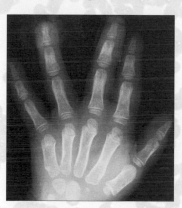

X-ray of a 2 ½-year-old hand

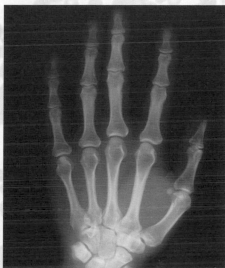

X-ray of an adult hand

SUPER PROTECTORS

Bones do more than just support the body. They also protect the soft organs inside. The following bones are some of those that act as armor for your organs.

Skull

The skull keeps the brain and sense organs safe from harm. The skull is made up of 26 different bones. The lower jaw and the tiny ear bones are the only bones in the skull that move. Did you know that your teeth are not bones? They are hard, bonelike structures. Teeth have a hard outer layer and a soft, pulpy inner layer.

The outer layer of a tooth is covered by a super-strong coating of *enamel,* which is the hardest substance in the human body.

Ribs

In your chest are 12 pairs of ribs. These ribs protect the heart, lungs, spleen, stomach, and liver. As you breathe in, your ribs move up and out. This helps your lungs take in more air.

Pelvis

The pelvis is made up of three bones. One is a bone at the base of the spine called the *sacrum.* The two other bones are the hip bones that make up the *pelvic girdle.* The pelvic girdle cradles and shields the intestines and the bladder.

THE FLEXIBLE SKELETON

Each bone in the human body is hard and unbending. Yet the skeleton itself is flexible. *Joints* make it possible for the skeleton to move. Joints are the places where two or more bones meet and allow movement. Some joints allow a lot of movement. Others move only a little or not at all.

Bones are held in place by *connective tissues. Cartilage* is a kind of connective tissue. It is found at the ends of the bones. Cartilage protects the bones and helps joints move smoothly. *Ligaments* are another type of connective tissue. They hold the bones together at the joints.

Bones don't move by themselves. Muscles move bones. Together bones and muscles allow movement to happen. How? *Tendons,* another type of connective tissue, connect muscles to bones. When a muscle *contracts,* or shortens, the tendons pull the bones, causing movement.

Some super-flexible parts of your body include the following.

Spine

The spine is the backbone of the body. The 26 bones in the spine are called *vertebrae.* They have cartilage in between them, allowing the spine to bend and twist.

Shoulder

The *scapula,* or shoulder blade, and the arm are connected by many muscles and ligaments. This flexible joint allows you to swing your arm in a full circle. Try it!

Hip

The *femur,* or thighbone, is the longest bone in your body. One end of it fits perfectly into your pelvis at your hip. The hip joint allows you to kick to the front and to the side.

Name That Bone

Sure, you can touch your kneecap, but can you point to your *patella*? Check out the scientific terms for some of the bones in your body.

Scapula—shoulder blade

Maxilla—upper jaw

Mandible—lower jaw

Clavicle—collarbone

Sternum—breastbone

Humerus, radius, ulna—arm bones

Femur, tibia, fibula—leg bones

Patella—kneecap

Phalanges—finger bones and toe bones

Coccyx—tailbone

Carpals—wrist bones

Tarsals—ankle bones

THE SHAPE OF YOUR SHAPE

Humans and many other animals have skeletons inside their bodies. The internal skeleton gives the body its shape. Without a skeleton, your body would be one big blob.

An animal's shape depends on its skeleton, too. Look at the skeletons below. Can you tell which animal skeletons they are?

a. b. c. d.

Shown are skeletons of a. an ostrich, b. a ferret, c. a horse, and d. a dog.

What's Inside Your Bones?

The bones in your body are living tissue. They are made mostly of calcium and protein. To stay strong, bones need oxygen, vitamins, and minerals. A good diet and plenty of exercise can help keep bones healthy and strong.

A bone is made up of several different parts. These parts include the following.

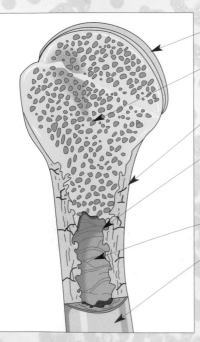

Hard Outer Layer: *The hard outer layer gives the bone its strength. It is made of dense, compact bone.*

Spongy Inner Layer: *The spongy inner layer makes the bone light. This same spongy material makes up the ends of the bone.*

Blood Vessels: *Blood vessels bring oxygen and other nutrients to the bone.*

Marrow Cavity: *The marrow cavity is the space in the center of the bone. It contains bone marrow. The marrow cavity is found only in long bones such as the leg and arm bones.*

Bone Marrow: *Bone marrow is a kind of tissue that makes blood cells. It is found in the marrow cavity of some bones.*

Periosteum: *The periosteum is a thin, tough layer that covers the bone surface.*

THE BROKEN RADIUS

"**I**saac Shearer," called the nurse from the doorway.

"Oh, no," Isaac groaned. He turned quickly to his mother. "Mom, I'm sure my arms will feel better if I give them some rest. My right arm doesn't hurt *too* much."

"Isaac, you might have broken one or both of your arms," Mom replied. "We need to have them checked out."

Isaac and his mother followed the nurse down the hall. The nurse stopped before a door marked *Radiology.* Inside the dark room, another hospital worker was waiting.

"Hi, Isaac," the man said. "I'm Dennis, your X-ray technician. I hear you had a bad spill on your skateboard. What I'm going to do is take pictures of your arms."

"Is this going to hurt?" Isaac asked nervously.

"No," Dennis assured him. "It will only take a few minutes. First I'll take pictures of your left arm. Then I'll take pictures of your right arm. We'll figure out if they're broken in no time."

Isaac followed Dennis's instructions. He climbed up on a table in the center of the room and lay down on it. Dennis covered him with a heavy apron. "This is to protect your body from the X-rays," Dennis explained. "When I take the picture, I'm going to leave the room. A little exposure to the X-rays is okay, but too many exposures could be unhealthy for me."

Isaac winced a little as the X-ray technician placed a tray under his left arm. "Okay, Isaac, hold very still now," Dennis said. Then he left the room.

After Dennis was done with Isaac's left arm, he X-rayed Isaac's right arm. Then Dennis led Isaac and his mother into another room to wait for Dr. Patel. In a little while, the doctor arrived. She was holding Isaac's X-rays under her arm. Isaac stared curiously as the doctor clipped the X-rays to a light box on the wall.

"Your mom was right, Isaac," Dr. Patel said. "You have a fractured left radius." She pointed to a spot on one of the X-rays that showed the break in Isaac's forearm bone.

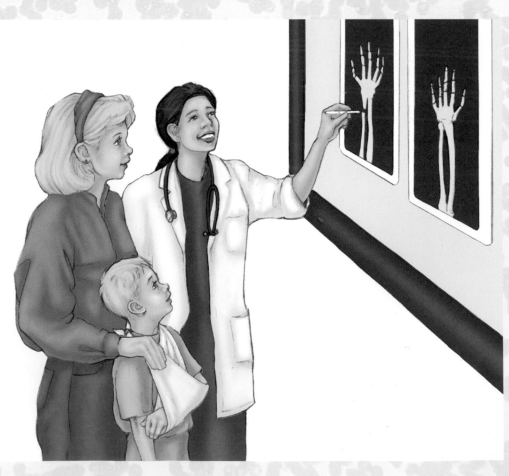

"Can you fix it?" Isaac asked.

"Absolutely," Dr. Patel replied. "Bones are living tissue. In fact, your arm has already started to heal itself." Then she pointed to the other X-ray. "The good news is that your right arm is fine. In about 6 weeks, you'll be out skateboarding again. With a little help from me, of course."

Dr. Patel smiled and began taking some materials from the shelves on the wall. "First we need to make sure your arm stays in the right place while it heals," she said. "So I'm going to put your arm in a fiberglass cast. The cast is light but very strong. You're lucky your break isn't too bad, Isaac. Some people need surgery to fix broken bones. They have to get wires, plates, and screws put in the bones to fix the fractures."

As Dr. Patel began fitting the cast onto Isaac's arm, Isaac stared at the X-rays on the light box. "That's pretty cool," Isaac said. "Is that what my arm looks like underneath my skin?"

"That's what your bone looks like," Dr. Patel explained. "There are also muscles and tendons under your skin that help you move your arms. But the X-ray is a kind of picture that shows only the bones."

Dr. Patel finished setting Isaac's broken arm. "You're all set," she said. "In a few weeks, we'll have another look. But for now, no more skateboarding. No other physical activities, either. And Isaac, I hope that the next time you get on your skateboard, you'll be a little more careful. I'm glad you were wearing a helmet. Now maybe you and your mom can pick up some wrist guards and knee and elbow pads."

"That's a good idea," said Isaac. "And the next time I go skateboarding, I'll stay away from that big hill!"

QUESTIONS TO EXPLORE

- What is the name of the bone that Isaac broke?
- For what reason was Isaac's arm put in a cast?
- For what reason might some bones be in a cast for a longer time than others?

The Boneyard

Take a break and bone up on these neat bone facts!

■ The smallest bones are found deep inside your ear. These bones are called the *malleus,* or "hammer," the *incus,* or "anvil," and the *stapes,* or "stirrup."

■ The *patella,* or kneecap, is unlike any other bone. This small, flat bone is not joined directly to any other bone. Instead it sits securely in a tendon on the front of the knee.

■ A newborn baby has about 300 "bones." Many of these bones are actually cartilage. The cartilage is replaced by true bone as the baby grows.

■ A baby's head is much more fragile than your own head. When a baby is born, its skull bones haven't grown together yet. So an infant has "soft spots." These areas are covered with membrane that will eventually be replaced by bone. During the first 2 years of a child's life, the skull bones fuse together, covering the soft spots. Where the bones meet, they form fixed joints called *sutures.* It takes between 20 and 40 years for the sutures to interlock completely.

■ Bones make up about 25 percent of your body's mass.

■ The first rib is the rib that is closest to your collarbone. It is shorter than the other ribs. It is also the flattest and most curved.

■ Bone marrow makes millions of blood cells every second.

■ The *clavicle,* or collarbone, is one of the most easily broken bones in the human body. It is often broken when a person falls on the shoulder, elbow, or outstretched arm. The force of such a fall damages the clavicle.

BARN OWLS

The barn owl swoops through the dark night. It flies low over a field. It scans the ground with its sensitive eyes and listens carefully with its large ears. Suddenly the barn owl spots its favorite prey. It is a vole, a small, mouselike animal. With one quick flap of its wings, the owl is upon the vole. It gobbles the tiny animal up in one bite. Without even touching the ground, the owl is off again. It has much more hunting to do before the night is over.

Barn owls are large birds with white, heart-shaped faces. They are found all over the world. Barn owls live near fields, pastures, and any places where voles and other small animals are found.

Barn owls swallow their prey whole. But they cannot digest the bones, fur, claws, and teeth of their prey. About 20 hours after feeding, barn owls *regurgitate,* or cough up, these bits. They come up as oval balls of fur and bones called "owl pellets." The pellets are about 3.75 to 7.5 centimeters (1.5 to 3 inches) long.

Barn owls don't tear or chew their prey. For this reason, the pieces of a complete skeleton of a small rodent can almost always be found in a pellet. Sometimes a pellet might contain the remains of several small animals. You can use a magnifying glass and toothpicks to pull a pellet apart. Then you can put together at least one skeleton of a barn owl's meal from the pellet.

A barn owl

A barn owl with prey in its mouth

9

YOUR AMAZING OPPOSABLE THUMB

You've got two! They're amazing! They are your opposable thumbs. The thumb is the key to how humans hold things. No other living thing has a hand and thumb exactly like yours. But what is an *opposable* thumb?

An opposable thumb allows you to touch the tip of your thumb to the tip of each finger. Try it! Then try to touch the tip of your index finger to the tip of your pinkie. Your fingers are designed to work together with your thumb. This allows you to use your hands in many different ways.

Because human thumbs work like this, we are able to pick up even tiny objects. We can hold things between the thumb and other fingers. This is called a *precision grip.* How important is your thumb? Try picking up a pen and writing without using your thumb.

What makes the thumb work the way it does? A unique gliding joint connects the thumb to the palm. This joint is called a *saddle joint.* The thumb is the only place the saddle joint is found. This joint allows the thumb to move side to side and back and forth. The human saddle joint is very strong.

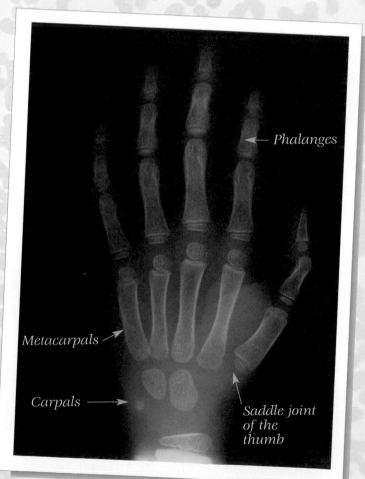

Phalanges

Metacarpals

Carpals

Saddle joint of the thumb

BONES ON THE OUTSIDE

Not all animals have skeletons on the inside. A very large number of animals called *arthropods* have skeletons on the outsides of their bodies. This kind of skeleton is called an *exoskeleton.* Exoskeletons are made of hard, thin tubes and plates. All animals with exoskeletons are *invertebrates,* or animals without backbones.

Scorpion

Tarantula

Clam

Crah

Who Am I?

Match each animal with its description.

1. Even the eyes of this spider are covered with a tough exoskeleton.

2. Like all arthropods, this aquatic animal must shed its exoskeleton to grow. It hides from its enemies while its new coat of armor hardens.

3. This land animal's exoskeleton has many different sections. Joints between the sections allow this animal to move easily.

4. This animal's exoskeleton creates a hard shell all around it. The two parts of the skeleton, called *valves,* are opened and closed by two big, strong muscles.

Bony Comparison

Which is better, bones on the outside or bones on the inside? You decide!

	Internal skeleton	Exoskeleton
Protection	Protects inner organs. Does not offer protection from enemies.	Protects inner organs. May offer protection from enemies.
Growth	Grows and expands with age.	Does not grow. Animal must shed exoskeleton to grow.
Movement	Works together with muscles and joints to allow for a variety of movements.	Plates and tubes of the exoskeleton are jointed. Inner muscles provide movement.

Answers: 1. Tarantula 2. Crab 3. Scorpion 4. Clam

COMPARING JOINTS

Some parts of the body are quite flexible. Others move only a little. That's because there are different types of joints in different places. There are more than 200 joints in the human body. Each has its own job to do. The shape of a joint determines exactly how that part of the body will move. In general, the less movement a body part has, the stronger that part of the body is.

A slippery, elastic tissue covers the ends of the bones where they meet and touch. This tissue is *cartilage.* The cartilage, kept slippery by a special fluid, allows the bones to move against one another with less friction.

Hinge Joint

Hinge joints are the most common types of joints in your body. A hinge joint works like the hinge of a door. It allows movement in only one direction. Hinge joints allow your legs, arms, and fingers to bend and straighten.

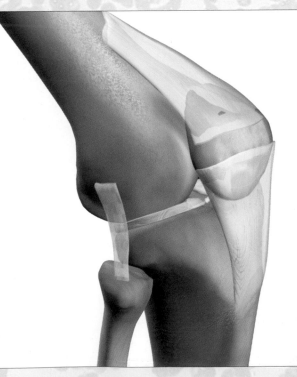

Hinge joints are found in the knees, elbows, fingers, and toes. The knee joint is the largest hinge joint in the human body. It "locks" when you stand straight. The knee joint's locking action makes it easier for you to stand for long periods of time.

Ball-and-Socket Joint

Ball-and-socket joints allow bones to swivel in nearly any direction. Ball-and-socket joints get their name from the shapes of the two bones that meet there. One example

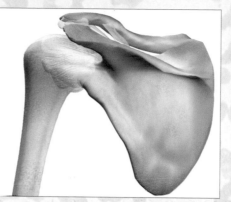

is the shoulder joint. The ball of the arm bone fits snugly into the hollow socket of the shoulder.

Ball-and-socket joints are found in the shoulder and hip. The hip is the strongest of all joints. It must be strong to support the weight of the upper body. It is not quite as flexible as the shoulder joint. You can swing your shoulder joint in a complete circle.

Gliding Joint

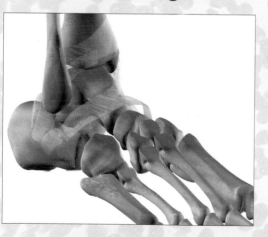

Gliding joints have two flat surfaces that glide smoothly and easily over one another. These joints allow only small movements. Gliding joints are found in the neck and spine, between pairs of vertebrae. Other gliding joints are found in the wrists and ankles.

QUESTIONS TO EXPLORE

- How is a hinge joint different from a ball-and-socket joint?
- How is a ball-and-socket joint different from a gliding joint?
- How is a gliding joint different from a hinge joint?

Interesting Animal Joints

Some animals have joints that are quite different from human joints.

Horse Horses have a joint called a *stifle joint* that is similar to the human knee. It can lock into place, allowing horses to stand for hours on end.

Gibbon In addition to having opposable thumbs, gibbons also have an opposable toe on each foot. This toe works like the opposable thumb. It allows the animal to hang onto branches with its feet while it travels from tree to tree.

Goat The goat and some other animals that eat plants have unusual jaw joints. Such a jaw joint allows the goat to move its jaw sideways, up and down, and front to back when chewing.

MUSCLES

Your body has more than 700 muscles. Without these muscles, you'd be going nowhere! Every move you make is powered by muscles. Muscles help you walk, run, and hit a baseball. When you blink, chew, or talk, you are using your muscles. Muscles also help keep your body upright and make your movements steady.

Muscles are made up of small, thick bundles of fibers. These fibers are designed for movement. When muscles *contract,* or shorten, they pull the bones, causing movement.

About 650 of your muscles are *skeletal muscles.* Skeletal muscles move the arms, legs, and other parts of the body. Skeletal muscles are also called *voluntary muscles.* That's because you can control these muscles. There are two other types of muscles. They are *smooth muscles* and *cardiac muscles.* Smooth muscles are found in the walls of blood vessels and some organs. Cardiac muscles are found in the walls of the heart.

MUSCLE PAIRS

Skeletal muscles nearly always work in pairs or groups. While one muscle contracts, the other relaxes. Look at your upper arm as you bend your arm at the elbow. The *biceps* and *triceps* muscles in your upper arm are working together. The biceps contracts and becomes shorter, while the triceps relaxes and becomes longer.

It's important to take care of your muscles. This means getting plenty of exercise and eating well. The more your muscles are used, the better they will work.

Muscles on the Move

Facial muscles: There are about 30 different muscles in your face. Most facial muscles are attached to each other or to the skin, not to bone. The facial muscles control a variety of movements. When you raise your eyebrows, wrinkle your forehead, close your eyes, or smile, your facial muscles are at work.

Neck muscles: Muscles in the neck must be very strong. They have to keep the head upright. An adult human head weighs about 4.5 kilograms (10 pounds).

Hand muscles: Each hand has about 20 different muscles. With so many muscles, the hand can move in a variety of ways.

Arm muscles: There are about 19 muscles in your lower arm alone. These muscles work with the hand muscles to make your wrists and fingers move.

Abdominal muscles: Your abdominal muscles allow you to twist and bend your body. They also help you inhale and exhale.

Gluteus maximus: The *gluteus maximus* is the largest muscle in your body. It is also one of the strongest. This big muscle helps you run, jump, and climb. It's also the muscle on which you sit!

Leg muscles: The muscles in your thigh bend, straighten, and twist both your hip and your knee. The muscles in your calf allow you to bend, straighten, and twist your ankle.

MUSCLES AND BONES: WORKING TOGETHER

Check out the muscles and bones that work together to make movement possible.

Gluteus Maximus–Thighbone and Pelvis

The *gluteus maximus* connects the *femur,* or thighbone, to the pelvic bones. This muscle controls running, climbing, and jumping.

Biceps and Triceps–Arm Bones

The *biceps* and *triceps* muscles help move the arm bones. The arm bones are the *humerus, radius,* and *ulna.* Bend your arm at the elbow, and the biceps contracts while the triceps relaxes. Straighten your arm, and the opposite happens.

Various Muscles–Shoulder Blade and Upper Arm Bone

The shoulder is one of the most flexible parts of the body. Many muscles are needed to hold the *scapula,* or shoulder blade, in place. The *deltoid* is one of the larger muscles in the shoulder area. This muscle helps raise the arm.

Calf Muscles–Heel Bone and Lower Leg Bones

The heel bone is connected to the calf muscles by the *Achilles tendon.* It is the longest and strongest tendon in your body. Calf and shin muscles also connect your lower leg bones, the *tibia* and *fibula,* to your ankle. These muscles help bend and straighten the ankle.

Neck Muscles–Skull and Spine

Pairs of muscles in your neck connect your skull to your spine. Each pair of muscles moves the skull in a different direction.

SPACE RACE

Think you'd like to be an astronaut? You've got a lot of hard work ahead of you. And that's before your shuttle ever blasts into space! Space missions can be hard on the human body. The astronauts who take part in these missions must be well trained and prepared. What does it take to be an astronaut?

Q: How do astronauts train physically and mentally for a flight?

A: To be an astronaut, you must first pass a number of tests. One type of test is a fitness test. Only people who are in tip-top shape are chosen. Of course, astronauts also must be well educated. Potential astronauts are given tests that measure their abilities to adapt, to get along with others, and to handle pressure. Once they pass the tests, astronauts begin to train. Their training

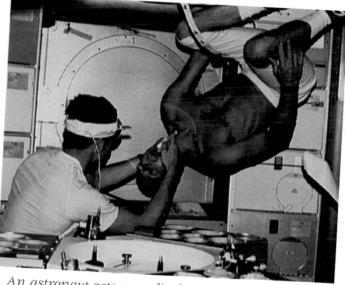

An astronaut gets a medical examination in space.

program is long and difficult. It can take several years. The training program helps astronauts prepare for spaceflights.

During training, astronauts must go to school. They attend classes and learn what they will need to know to fly space missions. They study textbooks and use computers as part of their training. They learn how to operate the space shuttles. They also practice any science experiments that will be performed during the flight. The more astronauts practice, the better prepared they are mentally for the mission ahead.

An important part of training is exercise. Astronauts need to stay fit and healthy for their spaceflights. They must also keep up good eating practices. This helps their bones, muscles, and other parts of their bodies stay strong. Jogging is just one of the exercises astronauts use to keep fit.

Astronauts also spend time in *simulators*. A simulator is any machine that copies conditions in space. For example, astronauts train in a special jet that lets them experience weightlessness. The jet flies the astronauts high into the sky. Then it dives thousands of meters. While the jet dives, astronauts are weightless. Then the jet climbs, and the astronauts do it all over again! Some astronauts become sick during the flight. That's why the jet is known as the "Vomit Comet."

Astronauts also take part in underwater training. They put on big, bulky spacesuits and jump into a giant pool. Being underwater is a lot like being in space. At the bottom of the pool, astronauts perform many different exercises. The exercises help them learn how to move in their spacesuits.

Training helps astronauts prepare for emergency situations. They are tested to make sure that they are mentally and physically ready for these situations. They are taught how to survive if their flight crashes in a forest, desert, or sea. Astronauts must be able to handle any problems that might arise during a flight.

An astronaut exercises while in space.

Q: **How do astronauts stay in shape during the weightlessness of spaceflight?**

A: Life in space is not like life on Earth. In space, objects have no weight. About half of all astronauts get "space sickness" during a flight. Space sickness causes the astronauts to feel sick to their stomachs. Space sickness is similar to motion sickness. Because astronauts are not used to weightlessness, their sense of balance is disturbed. Space sickness usually passes after 2 to 3 days.

Weightlessness can also cause the human body to change. Researchers study just how the body is affected during a spaceflight. They have learned that the muscles, bones, and heart are all affected by space travel.

In space, astronauts use their muscles less. There is no effect of gravity to put constant pressure on the muscles, either. So in space, muscles start to weaken. After a while, they begin to waste away. Muscles can be damaged in other ways, too. They begin to lose blood vessels and nerve connections. Bones are also affected in space. Astronauts lose calcium from their bodies, which causes their bones to shrink.

Exercise on long spaceflights is important. It helps control some of the damage to muscles, bones, and other parts of the body due to weightlessness. Exercise keeps astronauts from suffering serious physical damage. It keeps the heart and tissues healthy during flights. Drinking plenty of liquids and eating well also help the astronauts stay healthy.

Most astronauts exercise for a minimum of 2 hours each day. Exercise equipment on a space shuttle includes a *treadmill*. A treadmill is a device

Muscle Facts

■ Muscles make up about 40 percent of your body mass. Bones make up about 25 percent, skin makes up 10 percent, and your brain is just 2 percent of your entire body mass.

■ The smallest muscles in your body are found in your inner ear. They move the smallest bones in your body, the hammer, anvil, and stirrup.

■ Your tongue is one of the strongest muscles in your body.

■ Muscles are 75 percent water.

■ A cramp happens when a muscle contracts on its own and stays contracted. This may happen if the muscle is not getting enough oxygen.

that allows the astronauts to practice walking and running. Some shuttle flights carry a rowing machine and a bike fastened securely to the floor. Astronauts use these machines to keep fit.

Did you know that astronauts usually grow 2 or 3 centimeters (0.8 to 1.2 inches) while they are in space? That's because the spine lengthens. The discs between the vertebrae are no longer squashed together by gravity. They stretch out, and the astronaut "grows." Once back on Earth, however, astronauts return to their usual heights.

Q: What happens to astronauts after a flight?

A: Once a space shuttle is on the ground again, astronauts must adjust to life on Earth. Even the simplest of tasks such as walking are difficult at first. Until their muscles get used to Earth's gravity once again, the astronauts can be wobbly. To make sure returning astronauts are healthy, they must go through more testing. The tests also ensure that their bodies are beginning to return to normal after the flight.

Astronaut Eileen M. Collins, pilot, space shuttle Atlantis

THE FROZEN MAN

Thousands of years ago, a shepherd went into the mountains to tend his flock. At the end of the day, a storm blew through the mountains. The wind whistled fiercely. Snow began to fall. The exhausted man found shelter between two big, rocky ridges. He lay down to rest, hoping to weather the storm. But the cold mountain air was too much. In a few hours, the man was dead. For the next 5,000 years, he lay undisturbed in a bed of ice and snow.

AN AMAZING FIND

In September 1991, a German couple was hiking through the Alps. They saw something poking out of the snow. They realized they had discovered a human body. The two quickly made their way to the base of the mountain. They notified the police, who returned and began digging up the body.

No one knew what an important find the two Germans had made. Days later, scientists at the University of Innsbruck in Austria began to examine the frozen corpse. They realized the body had been lying in the ice for thousands of years. Soon the body became known as the "Iceman." Because it was found in the part of the mountains known as the Ötztal Alps, the body was also nicknamed "Oetzi."

Written for Kid-O-Graphic Magazine by Professor I. C. Mann

STUDYING THE ICEMAN

First the excited scientists carefully examined the Iceman's clothes and tools. They found that the man was wearing simple clothing made of grass and leather when he died. He was carrying a bow and arrows, an ax, a net, and a dagger. He was also carrying a mushroom. The scientists thought the mushroom was used as a germ-killing medicine.

ANTHROPOLOGISTS

Anthropologists are scientists who study how humans have lived through the ages. Anthropologists study fossil remains and artifacts. They also study what people look like and how they act in their daily lives. Anthropologists helped to examine the Iceman. An anthropologist created the model of the Iceman's head.

Next scientists set to work examining the body itself. In his frozen bed, the Iceman had been well preserved. Somehow all the moisture had been removed from his body. He had been "freeze-dried." The Iceman's body weighed just 13 kilograms (29 pounds) when it was discovered!

The Iceman's skin was like leather. It was tough and brown. As they examined it more closely, the scientists discovered faint tattoos. Most were groups of parallel lines. One, behind the Iceman's right knee, was shaped like a cross.

The scientists were even more amazed when they looked at the joints below the skin. The tattoos were located directly above places where the Iceman's joints had worn down. This made them think the tattoos were a kind of early medicine. The Iceman may have thought the tattoos would ease his pain.

WHO WAS THE ICEMAN?

Many people wanted to know more about the Iceman. How old was he? What did he look like? To find the answers, scientists gave the frozen corpse a complete physical exam.

To learn how old the Iceman was when he died, researchers first looked at his teeth. As people age, their teeth become worn down. Scientists also used

X-rays to examine the man's skull for signs of sutures. Since sutures take between 20 and 40 years to interlock completely, they could give a clue to the Iceman's age. The scientists determined the man had been about 45 years old when he died. The scientists measured the Iceman's femur. This told them he had been between 155 and 160 centimeters (62 and 64 inches) tall. He may have weighed about 49.5 kilograms (110 pounds).

One scientist looked at pictures of the Iceman's head and skull. Using the pictures, he created a model of what the man might have looked like when he was alive. The scientist believed the man had a thick lower lip, a wide forehead, and a large nose. The model had brown hair and blue eyes.

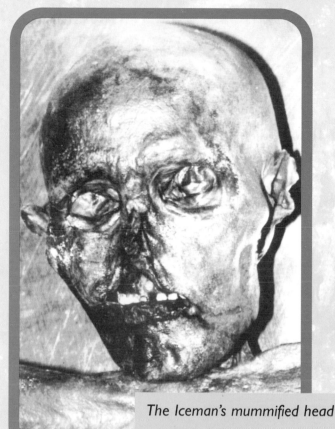
The Iceman's mummified head

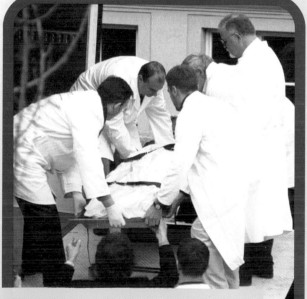
Scientists examining the body of the Iceman

BRONZE AGE OR STONE AGE?

At first, scientists had thought the Iceman was about 4,000 years old. The Iceman had an ax that the scientists thought was made of bronze. This would have placed the Iceman in the Bronze Age. The Bronze Age was a period of time that occurred around 2000 B.C.E.

To find out if the Iceman had lived during the Bronze Age, scientists performed a test. They took a piece of the Iceman's hip bone and tested it for a substance called *carbon 14*. Carbon 14 is a form of the element carbon that is present in all living things.

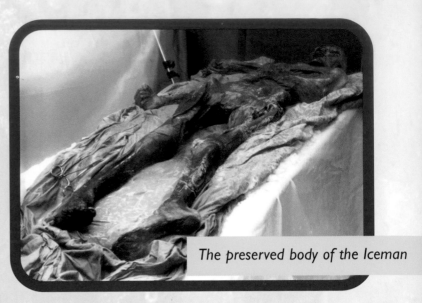

The preserved body of the Iceman

Scientists tested for the number of carbon 14 atoms in the Iceman's bone. From the carbon 14, they learned that the Iceman had lived about 5,300 years ago. This meant that the Iceman was from the Stone Age, not the Bronze Age. More testing showed that the ax was made of copper, not bronze. Bronze was used at a later time, after people had learned to melt copper and tin together to make the stronger metal. The Iceman is the oldest and best preserved human body ever discovered!

Scientists hope to learn even more about the Iceman. Today the body is kept in Italy, stored in a cold room. The room has the same conditions as an icy glacier. But even in this room, scientists can only study the Iceman for short periods of time. Every time someone examines the body, it begins to melt and decay. Scientists want to save the body for future study.

QUESTIONS TO EXPLORE

- **How do scientists think the Iceman became frozen?**
- **How do scientists date the ages of bones when they find them?**
- **Can you name three things that scientists learned about the Iceman?**

SMART TRAINING

What does it take to become a winning athlete? A lot of hard work, practice, and smart training.

BUILDING BETTER BODIES

Winning athletes need to take good care of their bodies. That's why they eat healthy foods. These foods are full of vitamins and nutrients that keep the body strong. A lot of fruits and vegetables are good for the entire body. Such foods as cheese, milk, and eggs are good for bones because they contain calcium and important vitamins. Other foods such as bread, rice, and pasta are good for muscles. These foods contain *carbohydrates*, nutrients that give the body energy.

Good sleep habits are also important to keep the body healthy. Athletes must get enough rest before a big race. Tired runners are not going to win the race. In fact, athletes might even risk injuries if they compete when they are tired. That's because their reactions are much slower when they are tired. Also, coordination is not as precise in tired athletes.

Athletes train on stairs to build muscles and endurance.

25

EXERCISE IS A MUST

Before any vigorous exercise, athletes must first stretch out. This loosens up the muscles and joints. It gets the body ready for the work ahead. Athletes who don't stretch out are more likely to get such injuries as cramps, strains, and tears. It is also important to stretch after a workout. During a race, an athlete's muscles tighten up. Stretching out afterwards loosens the muscles again.

To become the best they can be, athletes must train constantly. Nobody starts out being the best. Athletes must work at it. The more athletes practice, the better their skill and coordination become. Hurdlers become quicker and nimbler with more practice. High jumpers and broad jumpers move up to bigger jumps as they become more skilled. Discus throwers can throw greater distances once they learn how to coordinate their body movements properly.

Athletes also know when to stop and take care of themselves. Aches, pains, and bruises can be signs of more serious injuries. Some common athletic injuries include the following.

Cramps

Cramps occur when muscles are tired, overstretched, or lacking oxygen or other nutrients.

Sprains

Sprains occur when ligaments are damaged. *Ligaments* are the tough bands that hold joints together. The ankle is one part of the body that is commonly sprained by athletes.

Strains

Strains occur when tendons or muscle tissues are damaged. *Tendons* are the tissues that connect muscles to bones. Strains happen when athletes are not properly warmed up before they exercise. When an athlete works too hard, he or she may strain the tendons around the knee. This type of strain is often called *tendonitis*.

Women marathoners at the 1997 World Cup race

THE RIGHT STUFF

One of the most important parts of training for a race is having a positive attitude. Runners win because they think they can. They become self-confident by practicing all the time. The more they practice certain skills, the better they get. The more skilled athletes become, the more positive they are that they can be the best.

Athletes are also determined to win. They don't give up when they lose a race or two. Winners learn from losing. They take what they've learned and try even harder the next time.

Most athletes have good attitudes because they enjoy what they do. Win or lose, they love to run, jump, or throw. This is why they compete.

THE CIRCULATORY SYSTEM

While you're busy running, jumping, or shooting a basketball, your body systems are hard at work. The *circulatory system*, for example, is automatically pumping blood through your body. The circulatory system delivers blood to all parts of the body. This system includes the heart, lungs, blood, and blood vessels.

The heart is one of the most important muscles in your body. It is a strong muscle about the size of a fist. Your heart works automatically. Once every second or so, the heart squeezes and relaxes. The heart never rests. People must eat healthy foods to take care of their hearts. Take good care of your heart by eating well, exercising, and getting plenty of rest.

The heart is made up of two separate pumps. The pump on the right side sends blood through the lungs. When blood travels through the lungs, it becomes rich in oxygen. The oxygen-rich blood then returns to the left side of the heart.

The pump on the left side sends the oxygen-rich blood throughout the rest of the body. The oxygen in the blood is used up by the body's cells and tissues. The oxygen-poor blood then returns to the right side of the heart.

BLOOD VESSELS

Blood is carried around the body through tubes known as *blood vessels*. There are three different types of blood vessels.

Arteries are thick blood vessels that carry blood quickly out of the heart and into the body. Arteries branch out from the heart, becoming capillaries.